Caribbea
Junior E

Haydn Richards with
Pamela Mordecai and
Grace Walker Gordon

CW00327426

Ginn and Company Ltd

Contents

The game of I spy

A   Do you know the game of **I Spy**?
Look at the first picture.
I spy with my little eye
Something beginning with **c**.

1   c__ __

This is a **cup**, so you write the word **cup**.
Now do the same with the other pictures.

2   p__ __   3   b__ __ __   4   s__ __ __

5   d__ __   6   l__ __   7   t__ __ __

8   f__ __ __   9   j__ __   10 e__ __

B   Which word fills the gap?

1   A hen laid the ___ .

2   The ___ can bark.

3   A ___ lives in water.

4   A ___ is worn on the foot.

Names of things

bag   drum
bed   lamp
book   pen
clock   spoon
door   tap

A   Write in order, 1 to 10, the names of the things in the pictures. Look at the list of words on the left.

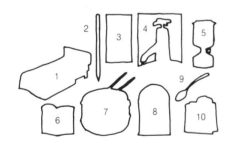

B   **What am I?**

1 You beat me with two sticks.

2 You lie on me when you go to sleep.

3 I can give light when it is dark.

4 You open me when you enter a room.

5 You carry your shopping in me.

6 You look at me when you read.

7 You come to me for water.

8 People use me to stir their tea.

9 You may use me when you write.

10 I tell you the time.

The words you have written are the **names** of things. We call such words **naming** words or **nouns**.

Using a and an

arrow   envelope
axe   iron
egg   onion
elephant   orange

A   Write the names of these things, putting **an** in front of each. The words you need are in the list on the left.

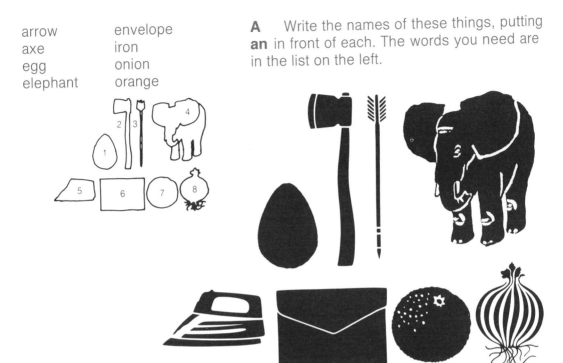

Always write **an** before words beginning with

a e i o u

Always write **a** before words beginning with other letters.

B   Write **a** or **an** before each of these words.

1 ___ clock

2 ___ armchair

3 ___ owl

4 ___ book

5 ___ pen

6 ___ arch

7 ___ tree

8 ___ door

9 ___ elephant

10 ___ ostrich

11 ___ eagle

12 ___ hoop

13 ___ desk

14 ___ island

15 ___ umbrella

Numbers

•   **1**
       one

Three cats
Draw five cats.

• •   **2**
      two

___ spoons
Draw four spoons.

• • •   **3**
       three

___ trees
Draw one tree.

• • • •   **4**
       four

___ car
Draw two cars.

• • • • •   **5**
       five

___ oranges
Draw three oranges.

• • •   **6**
• • •   **six**

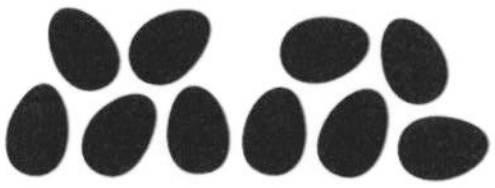

___ eggs
Draw seven eggs.

• • • •   **7**
• • •   **seven**

___ flowers
Draw nine flowers.

• • • •   **8**
• • • •   **eight**

___ pencils
Draw ten pencils.

• • • • •   **9**
• • • •   **nine**

___ mugs
Draw eight mugs.

• • • • •   **10**
• • • • •   **ten**

___ bottles
Draw six bottles.

4

Doing words

eating   playing
drinking   reading
fishing   sleeping
flying   washing
jumping

A What are they **doing**?
Make a list of the **doing** words. Number them from 1 to 9.

B Write the word which fills each gap.

1 The man is ___ his van.

2 The boy is ___ under the tree.

3 The two boys are ___ .

4 The girl is ___ an orange.

5 Her friend is ___ .

6 The woman is ___ a book.

7 The dog is ___ over a log.

8 The birds are ___ high.

9 The girls are ___ ball.

C Add **-ing** to each of these words.

1	call	5	pull	9	sing
2	draw	6	see	10	bark
3	do	7	hear	11	teach
4	try	8	rain	12	feel

5

Pam's pet

Pam's pet is a cat named Cindy. She has a long fluffy tail. It looks like a powder puff. She licks it every day to keep it clean. She holds it high in the air when she walks.

Cindy is a very proud cat. She likes to get her own food. She catches mice and lizards. After she eats she washes her face with her soft paws. Her claws are very sharp, but she never scratches Pam. Cindy often goes for a walk with Pam.

Copy the sentences.
Fill each space with the right word.

1 Pam's pet is a ＿＿ called ＿＿ .

2 Her tail looks like a ＿＿ ＿＿ .

3 She ＿＿ it every day to keep it ＿＿ .

4 She holds it ＿＿ in the air.

5 Cindy is a ＿＿ cat.

6 She catches her own ＿＿ .

7 Her claws are ＿＿ .

8 She never ＿＿ Pam.

More doing words

A   Look at the picture.
Make a list of the **doing** words. Number them
from 1 to 8.

When **-ing** is added to a
doing word ending with **e**,
the **e** is dropped.

B   Use the words in the list on the left to fill
these gaps.

dance	dancing
dive	diving
hide	hiding
ride	riding
skate	skating
smoke	smoking
wave	waving
write	writing

1 Errol likes ____ his father's donkey.

2 Ben is ____ in the bushes.

3 Pam is ____ to us across the road.

4 Angela uses pen and ink when she is ____ .

5 The old man is ____ a pipe.

6 Michael enjoys ____ off the pier.

7 Shirley likes to do folk ____ .

8 The children are ____ on the sidewalk.

Telling sentences

Read this sentence.

A cat has sharp claws.

This sentence tells us something about a cat.

It is called a **telling** sentence.

Every **telling** sentence must end with a **full stop**.

A Copy these sentences and put a **full stop** at the end of each.

1 Butter is made from milk
2 Honey is made by bees
3 Somebody loves you
4 You are an important person
5 They need your help
6 I put some coal on the fire
7 We pick ripe mangoes from the tree
8 Cool breezes blow at Christmas time
9 I feel free up in this tree
10 These mangoes are juicy

B Now write one **telling** sentence about each of these things.

1 a cow
2 your home
3 a tree
4 coal
5 your toys
6 a bird

Asking sentences

Some sentences ask a question.

What is your name?

How old are you?

Where do you live?

Every **asking** sentence must end with a **question mark**.

A   Copy these sentences and put a **question mark** at the end of each.

1   How are you today

2   Do you like to sing

3   Why is he smiling

4   When are you coming to see me

5   Who planted this big pumpkin vine

6   Which of these toys do you like best

7   Will you come to the post office with me

8   Did you remember to post the letter

9   Have you seen John

10   Can you tell me the way

B   Now write one **asking** sentence about each of these things.

1   the time   4   a farm

2   the weather   5   money

3   a book   6   clothes

Capital letters beginning a sentence

Every sentence, both **telling** and **asking**, must begin with a **capital letter**.

Small letters   a b c d e f g h i j
Capital letters   A B C D E F G H I J

A   Copy these sentences.
Begin each with a capital letter.

Put a **full stop** at the end of each **telling** sentence.

Put a **question mark** at the end of each **asking** sentence.

1   corn is good for you

2   we grow corn in our yard

3   do you grow corn

4   hens lay eggs

5   eggs break easily

6   will you help to carry them

7   please be careful

8   this basket is full of eggs

9   look where you are going

10 what do you feed the hens with

B   Write six sentences about the goat.
Say something about –

1   its hair   4   its horns

2   its ears   5   its beard

3   its tail   6   its food

The alphabet

This is the alphabet.

You should learn the alphabet well.

From these twenty-six letters all our words are made.

a b c d e f g h i j k l m
n o p q r s t u v w x y z

A

1 What is the fifth letter?

2 Write the last letter of all.

3 Which letter comes after **s**?

4 Which letter comes just before **h**?

5 Write the letter which comes between **k** and **m**.

6 Write the two letters on either side of **e**.

7 Which letter is next but one after **q**?

8 Which is the letter but one before **j**?

9 What are the missing letters?
  m n — p q r — t u — w x

10 What word do the missing letters spell?
  a — c d — f — h

These letters are jumbled up:
c e a d b

Now they are in the right **a b c** order:
a b c d e

B Place the letters below in **a b c** order.

1 n p o l m

2 v y w u x

3 q r u t v s

4 d f b a e c

5 i k h g f j

The Henry family

Use the words in the list on the left to fill the gaps in these sentences.

ball
banana
book
cat
family
five
floor
girl
hands
letter
mother
radio
rug

1 This is the Henry ___ .

2 There are ___ people in all.

3 The father is reading a ___ .

4 He is also eating a ___ .

5 The ___ is writing a ___ .

6 The baby is sitting on the ___ .

7 She has a ___ in her ___ .

8 The ___ is playing with the ___ .

9 The dog is asleep on the ___ .

10 The boy is listening to the ___ .

Doing words

When we add **-ing** to some doing words we **double the last letter**.

bat	batting
chop	chopping
clap	clapping
cut	cutting
run	running
sit	sitting
skip	skipping
swim	swimming

A   Make a list of the **doing** words which fit these pictures.
Number them from 1 to 8.

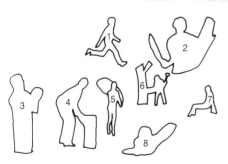

B   Fill the gap in each sentence by adding **-ing** to the word in bold type at the end of each line. Remember to double the last letter first.

1   Colin kept ___ on the wet floor.   **slip**

2   Tony enjoyed ___ in the garden.   **dig**

3   The bus will be ___ at the school gates.   **stop**

4   We shall be ___ off there.   **get**

5   The guavas lay ___ on the ground.   **rot**

6   I am ___ my toys away.   **put**

7   Roy went out without ___ the door.   **shut**

8   Carol was ___ her dog.   **pat**

Capital letters

This girl's name is Ruth Ann Brown.

The name of her pet cat is Skipper.

The girl's last name, **Brown**, is her **surname**.

Her other names, **Ruth Ann**, are her **Christian names** or **first names**.

The names of people and pets always begin with a **capital letter**.

A Write your first names and your surname.

Now write out these sentences, using **capital letters** for the names of people and pets.

1 I told mary that I would play with her after dinner.

2 When carmen fell down paul helped her up.

3 I think david biggs is taller than john morgan.

4 The names of the twins are pamela and kenneth.

5 I saw leroy young feeding his dog sam.

6 We saw daisy the cow being milked.

7 linda named her new donkey sunshine.

8 The name of our cat is fluffy.

The word **I** is always a capital letter.

What shall **I** have to eat?

B Write a capital **I** in each space.

1 Where did ___ put my comb?

2 Do you think ___ am tall for my age?

3 Marion said ___ could have an orange.

4 ___ think ___ have a cold coming on.

5 When ___ am tired ___ lie down and rest.

14

Names and initials

Mr. Brown   Mrs. Brown   Miss James   Dr. Baker

The name of Ruth's father is Mr. Norman Brown.

Her mother's name is Mrs. June Brown.

The name of Ruth's teacher is Miss Freda James.

The family doctor is Dr. John Baker.

Instead of writing a person's first name, we sometimes write only the first letter.

For **Richard** we write **R**.

For **Mary** we write **M**.

We call these letters **initials**.

Initials are always followed by a **full stop**.

Mr. is a short way of writing **Mister**.

Mrs. is a short way of writing **Missis**.

There is no short way of writing **Miss**.

Dr. is a short way of writing **Doctor**.

Write these names the short way, using initials for the first names.

A
1 Mister John Jones
2 Mister Henry Simpson
3 Mister Percy Lee

B
1 Missis Carmen Brown
2 Missis Doreen Gray
3 Missis Joy Ann Davis

C
1 Miss Jennifer Mason
2 Miss Dorothy Allen
3 Miss Anna Nandrani Persaud

D
1 Doctor Rohan Khan
2 Doctor Howard Taylor
3 Doctor Winston Chin

More than one

one chick   two chick**s**

one goat   three goat**s**

A   Write the missing words.

four ___   two ___   five ___

three ___   seven ___   six ___

B   Copy these **naming** words.
Write **s** after each to make it mean **more
than one**.

1	hen	5	duck	9	nut
2	cow	6	cat	10	sweet
3	ship	7	boat	11	cap
4	pen	8	sock	12	shoe

C   What are the missing words?

1   one dog   four ___

2   one leg   two ___

3   one girl   five ___

4   one week   three ___

5   one day   six ___

6   a sweet   a bag of ___

7   a chocolate   a box of ___

8   a card   a pack of ___

9   a book   many ___

10   a boy   a few ___

Numbers: the teens

one and ten = **eleven**   **11**

two and ten = **twelve** (dozen)   **12**

three and ten = **thirteen**   **13**

four and ten = **fourteen**   **14**

five and ten = **fifteen**   **15**

six and ten = **sixteen**   **16**

seven and ten = **seventeen**   **17**

eight and ten = **eighteen**   **18**

nine and ten = **nineteen**   **19**

teen means **and ten**

1   Which word means three and ten?

2   Dozen is another name for ___ .

3   ___ is one less than twelve.

4   The last teen number is ___ .

5   The number ___ is seven more than ten.

6   William is now fourteen years old.
    He will be ___ on his next birthday.

7   Sheila had ten red beads and four blue ones.
    She had ___ altogether.

8   After Eric had lost one of his nineteen marbles he had ___ left.

9   ___ is twice as big as six.

10 Write the word for 16.

11 Write the words for the four even numbers in the list.

12 Write the words for the five odd numbers in the list.

Verses

A Read the verses. Then do the exercises.

What Does the Bee Do?

What does the bee do?
  Bring home honey.
What does father do?
  Bring home money.
What does mother do?
  Count the money.
And what does baby do?
  Eat up the honey.

1 ___ counts the money.
2 Baby eats up the ___ .
3 The ___ brings home honey.
4 ___ brings the money home.

B

Go to bed early . . wake up with joy;
Go to bed late . . . cross girl or boy.
Go to bed early . . ready for play;
Go to bed late . . . moping all day.
Go to bed early . . no pains or ills;
Go to bed late . . . doctors and pills.
Go to bed early . . grow very tall;
Go to bed late . . . stay very small.

1 When you go to bed ___ you are ready for play.
2 To grow very tall you must ___ ___ ___ ___ .
3 If you go to bed late you will be ___ all day.
4 Children who go to bed early have no ___ or ___ .
5 How do children who go to bed early wake up?

He and she

A **boy** is a **he**.

A **girl** is a **she**.

He	She
boy	girl
brother	sister
bull	cow
cock	hen
father	mother
grandfather	grandmother
husband	wife
king	queen
man	woman
nephew	niece
prince	princess
uncle	aunt

A   Learn the words in the list on the left, then write the words which are missing from each sentence.

1   David's grandmother and ___ are very old.

2   James spent a holiday with his uncle and ___ .

3   There is work to do for every man and ___ .

4   Tony took his ___ and niece to the museum.

5   Both husband and ___ like farming.

6   The king and ___ ruled for many years.

7   Bob and Pam are brother and ___ .

8   The cock has a comb but the ___ does not.

B   Give the missing words.

1   ___ and wife

2   ___ and girl

3   ___ and aunt

4   ___ and niece

5   ___ and sister

6   ___ and cow

7   ___ and mother

8   ___ and queen

19

Days of the week

1 Sunday

2 Monday

3 Tuesday

4 Wednesday

5 Thursday

6 Friday

7 Saturday

The name of every day of the week begins with a **capital letter**.

Learn the names of the days and the order in which they come.

Sunday to Sunday

Watch and pray on Sunday,
Wash all day on Monday,
Iron clothes on Tuesday,
Clean the house on Wednesday,
To the store on Thursday,
Market day is Friday,
Saturday is fun day,
Then another Sunday.

Grace Walker-Gordon and Pamela Mordecai

Write the name of the day which will fill each gap in these sentences.

1 If today is Wednesday, yesterday was ___ .

2 Which day of the week has most letters in its name?

3 The school is closed on ___ and ___ .

4 ___ comes between Wednesday and Friday.

5 The day before Thursday is ___ .

6 Jesus rose from the dead on the first Easter ___ .

7 On ___ many people go to church.

8 If today is Friday, then tomorrow will be ___ .

9 Which day has in its name a letter **d** which is silent?

10 Sunday is the first day of the week. Which is the last day?

More than one

one box   two box**es**

We add **-es** to box to show
more than one.

A   Write the missing words.
Each ends with **-es**.

1   one bush   four ___
2   one watch   six ___
3   one brooch   two ___
4   one brush   five ___
5   one box   nine ___
6   one mango   a dish of ___
7   a dish   a set of ___
8   a church   a few ___
9   a stitch   many ___
10   a match   a box of ___

one bus   three bus**es**

We add **-es** to bus to show
more than one.

B   Use the words you have made to fill
these gaps.

1   The jeweller sold many different clocks
and ___ .
2   There were lots of prickles on the ___ .
3   Many ___ have a cross on their building.
4   Janet dropped the ___ on the floor.
5   The man used four ___ to light the fire.
6   Grandmother sometimes wears two ___ .
7   Garfield got the ___ to clean his shoes.
8   We gave our teacher two ___ of chocolates.
9   The children picked a basket full of ___ .
10   At the hospital Lance got six ___ in his
forehead.

Capital letters

Look at this address.

The **name of the street** begins with a **capital letter**.

The **name of the town** begins with a **capital letter**.

The **name of the country**, begins with a **capital letter**.

The names of places always begin with a **capital letter**.

> Miss Carmen Morgan,
> 24 Main Street,
> Kingstown,
> St. Vincent

A Write these sentences, using capital letters for the names of all places. End each sentence with a full stop.

1 One of the largest islands in the west indies is cuba

2 Ships sail from kingston

3 He was born in nassau

4 georgetown is a very old city

5 Marion lives in belmont road, port-of-spain

6 We went by boat to montserrat

7 The liner docked in bridgetown

8 The widest river in guyana is the essequibo

9 Asphalt comes from the pitch lake in trinidad

10 There is a large oil refinery in curaçao

B

1 Write your own name and address.

2 Write the name and address of any friend.

3 Write the name and address of any relation.

Two and too

Two and **too** have a similar sound.

He has **too** many boxes.
(more than enough)

They are very big, **too**.
(also)

The **two** pigs

Each has **two** ears

Two and **too** have different meanings.

Write **two** or **too** in each space below.

1 Alan went to bed ___ late.

2 ___ and ___ make four.

3 He is ___ ill to go to school.

4 It is nearly ___ o'clock.

5 Are you coming to the party ___ ?

6 I am going to buy ___ coconuts.

7 It is ___ hot to play games outside.

8 The ___ girls were great friends.

9 Is Grandpa on the ___ o'clock bus?

10 Jim is getting ___ fat.

Busy children

boys   standing
books   painting
five   crayons
front   picture
girls   cat
jar   showing
Ann   table
Errol   Ranjit
Lloyd   Mary

Look at the picture carefully.
Use the words in the list on the left to fill the gaps in the sentences.

1   There are ___ children in the picture.

2   Two of them are ___ and three are ___ .

3   ___ has made a ___ out of clay.

4   ___ has done a drawing and is ___ it to Lloyd.

5   There is a ___ of water in ___ of ___ .

6   ___ is ___ a ___ of a house.

7   Her picture is leaning against some ___ .

8   ___ has a set of ___ .

9   She sits at one end of the ___ .

10   Ann is the only child ___ by the window.

24

Numbers: the tens

20 **twenty** means **two tens**

30 **thirty** means **three tens**

40 **forty** means **four tens**

50 **fifty** means **five tens**

60 **sixty** means **six tens**

70 **seventy** means **seven tens**

80 **eighty** means **eight tens**

90 **ninety** means **nine tens**

100 **hundred** means **ten tens**

Ann

A   Write the words which fill the gaps.

1 Seven tens are ____ .

2 The number ____ is one half of a hundred.

3 Four times ten are ____ .

4 Six rows of ten make ____ .

5 Three tens are ____ .

When we write a **units** word after a **tens** word we use a hyphen **-**.

six tens and four units
sixty and four
sixty-four

B   Write the words for –

a   42

b   97

c   78

d   54

e   83

f   two tens and nine units

g   nine tens and four units

h   eight tens and five units

i   three tens and eight units

Colours

Look at the list of colours below.

Learn how to spell each word, then answer the questions.

black
blue
brown
green
grey
red
white
yellow

A   What is the colour of:

1   butter
2   grass
3   tar
4   the sea
5   chocolate
6   a poinsettia
7   a ripe banana
8   rainclouds
9   a ripe tomato
10 a polar bear

B   Write the name of anything which is:

1   black
2   white
3   red
4   green
5   yellow

C   Write these sentences, putting in the missing words.

1   After the rainy season the leaves on the trees are ___ .

2   When the traffic light is ___ the traffic must stop.

3   When the traffic light is ___ the traffic can go.

4   Butter is ___ in colour.

5   Most brides wear ___ dresses.

6   On a sunny day the sky is ___ .

7   A lump of coal is ___ in colour.

8   When bread is toasted it turns ___ .

9   Most fire engines are bright ___ .

10 When people get old their hair turns ___ or ___ .

More than one

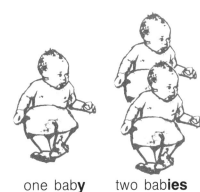

one bab**y**   two bab**ies**

one pupp**y**   four pupp**ies**

To make the words **baby** and **puppy** mean **more than one** we change the **y** to **i** before adding **-es**.

baby   puppy
babi   puppi
babies   puppies

A   Now do the same with these words which end with **y**.

1 fly   a swarm of ___

2 pony   two ___

3 puppy   a litter of ___

4 cherry   a bunch of ___

5 factory   two ___

6 country   several ___

7 story   a book of ___

8 fairy   many ___

9 baby   four ___

10 lady   a few ___

B   Use the words you have made to fill these gaps.

1 The ___ were so good that I ate all of them.

2 Some old ___ are very lively.

3 Our dog had four ___ today.

4 Three ___ were grazing in the field.

5 David likes to read ___ about animals.

6 In some Caribbean ___ the people speak French.

7 Several ___ were buzzing round the jam.

8 Do you believe in ___ ?

More than one

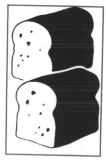

one loa**f**   two loa**ves**

one lea**f**   three lea**ves**

To make the words **loaf**
and **leaf** mean **more than
one**, we change the **f** to **v**
before adding **-es**.

loaf	leaf
loav	leav
loaves	leaves

A   Now do the same with these words.

1   thief   ten ___

2   shelf   three ___

3   loaf   five ___

4   half   two ___

5   calf   six ___

6   leaf   many ___

7   hoof   four ___

8   wolf   a pack of ___

With these words, change the **f** to **v** and add
-s. The **e** is there already.

9   wife ___

10 life ___

11 knife ___

B   Use the words you have made to fill
these gaps.

1   The ___ in the shop were full of toys.

2   The baker had only three ___ of bread left.

3   The ___ of banana trees are very large.

4   There are two ___ in one whole.

5   Baby cows are called ___ .

6   A horse has four ___ .

7   The butcher has very sharp ___ .

8   The police caught the car ___ .

Adding -ed to doing words

To make a **doing** word
show **past time** we add **-ed**

Now	Past
Today I play	Yesterday I played
Today I work	Last week I worked

A Add **-ed** to each of these **doing** words.

1	rain	6	bark
2	play	7	fill
3	chew	8	pick
4	wait	9	open
5	ask	10	fetch

Use the words you have made to fill the gaps in these sentences.

1 Last week Jane ___ her mother for more lunch money.

2 Lloyd ___ a grapefruit off the tree this morning.

3 Yesterday the dog ___ at the postman.

4 Kamla ___ the paper for her parents.

5 The kitten ___ with the ball until it fell asleep.

6 On Monday morning the man ___ one hour for the bus.

7 Terry ___ the bucket with water and took it into the house.

8 It ___ last night.

9 The cow ___ the grass for a long time.

10 He ___ the door and went in.

Peter's toys

Peter is very clever with his hands. He has lots of toys and he makes most of them himself. Sometimes his cousin Alan helps him.

Peter makes boats from bits of wood and paints them in bright colours. Some are steam ships. Some are oil tankers. Some are little sail boats. He gives them names like "Arawak Queen" and "Rising Sun" and "Go and Come Back".

Peter has cars and trucks made from boxes of all kinds. He uses cotton reels or bottle tops for wheels. He has a firehouse made from cardboard cartons. He even has a toy crane that can lift things!

1 Peter makes most of his ＿＿ himself.

2 He makes ＿＿ from ＿＿ of wood.

3 He paints them in ＿＿ colours.

4 Some are steam ＿＿ ; some are ＿＿ tankers and some are ＿＿ sail boats.

5 He has ＿＿ and ＿＿ made from boxes.

6 He uses cotton ＿＿ or bottle ＿＿ for wheels.

7 He has a firehouse made from cardboard ＿＿ .

8 He even has a ＿＿ crane that can ＿＿ things.

Using is and are/Using was and were

The tree **is** bare.
We use **is** for **one** tree.

The trees **are** bare.
We use **are** for **more than one**.

We use **was** for one person or thing.

We use **were** for more than one person or thing.

A   Fill each space with **is** or **are**.

1   This orange ___ sour.
    These oranges ___ sour.

2   ___ the house old?
    ___ the houses old?

3   The dog ___ barking.
    The dogs ___ barking.

4   ___ the egg fresh?
    ___ the eggs fresh?

B   Fill each space with **was** or **were**.

1   One egg ___ cracked.
    Three eggs ___ cracked.

2   The girl ___ skipping.
    The girls ___ skipping.

3   ___ the mango ripe?
    ___ the mangoes ripe?

4   The cow ___ being milked.
    The cows ___ being milked.

C   Choose the right word from the pair above to fill each space.

1   **is   are**
    Mother ___ ill, but Father ___ well.

2   **was   were**
    The hens ___ laying, so the farmer ___ pleased.

3   **was   were**
    The sea ___ rough and the waves ___ high.

4   **is   are**
    School ___ over and we ___ going home.

5   **was   were**
    They ___ glad because the day ___ sunny.

The alphabet

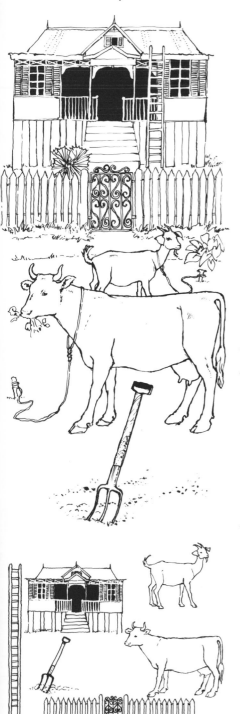

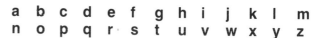

a b c d e f g h i j k l m
n o p q r s t u v w x y z

A   Write the names of the things in the picture in **a b c** order.

B   Write each line of words below in **a b c** order.

Example

us   go   on   he   am   is

Written in alphabetical order:

am   go   he   is   on   us

1 if   be   an   pan   so   do

2 day   fat   car   add   end   big

3 one   two   bit   job   low   son

4 why   bag   got   arm   eye   use

C   In each group below all the words are in **a b c** order except one. Can you spot the odd word?

In group 1 below the odd word is **gun**

1 arm	2 hat	3 bed	4 fat	5 queen
ball	zoo	ear	goat	ring
can	jar	kid	hut	bell
deer	log	net	wet	tray
gun	man	pad	ink	use
egg	peg	cow	jug	van
fan	rat	sun	king	web

32

Doing words: past time

To make a **doing** word show
past time we add **-ed**.

Now	Past
Today I play	Yesterday I play**ed**.
Today I work	Last week I work**ed**.

But if the **doing** word ends
with **e**, we just add **-d**.

The snails move slowly.   The snails move**d** slowly.

A   Make each of these **doing** words show
past time by adding **-d**.

1	sneeze	5	hope	9	save
2	like	6	wave	10	lace
3	wipe	7	use	11	bake
4	smoke	8	dive	12	move

B   Make the word to fill each space by
adding **-d** to the word in bold type.

1 Peter ___ loudly.   **sneeze**

2 They ___ to Kingston last week.   **move**

3 The Prime Minister ___ to the crowd.   **wave**

4 The old man ___ a long thin pipe.   **smoke**

5 The sailor ___ into the rough sea.   **dive**

6 Mother ___ all the flour to make a cake.
use

7 I have ___ fifty cents this week.   **save**

8 Shirley ___ having rotis for lunch.   **like**

9 Ann ___ the baby's mouth.   **wipe**

10 Peter ___ his shoes himself.   **lace**

Adding -ed to doing words

When we add **-ed** to some
doing words we **double the
last letter**.

Double the last letter.	rob	tug
Add on **-ed**.	rob**b**	tug**g**
	rob**bed**	tug**ged**

A   Add **-ed** to each of these doing words.
Remember to double the last letter.

1	pin	6	hug
2	clap	7	wag
3	stop	8	chop
4	beg	9	hum
5	rap	10	sip

B   Use the words you have made to fill
the gaps in these sentences.

1   The little dog ___ for a bone.

2   He ___ his tail when he got it.

3   Betty ___ the hot tea slowly.

4   The bus ___ outside the school.

5   Paula ___ her new teddy bear.

6   Garfield ___ at the door before going in.

7   Carol ___ her school badge on to her uniform.

8   The scouts ___ the wood for the fire.

9   The children ___ their hands for joy.

10   A swarm of bees ___ round our heads.

34

Putting sentences in order

Here are four short stories.
The sentences in them are in the wrong order.
Write them as they should be.

1 a He paid the shopkeeper.

   b He joined his friends outside.

   c James went into the sweet shop.

   d He put the change in his pocket.

   e He asked for a packet of mints.

2 a She drank all the milk.

   b She put a straw in the bottle.

   c She put the empty bottle in the crate.

   d Shanta took a bottle of milk from the crate.

   e She took off the cap.

3 a He went to the bathroom.

   b He went off to catch the school bus.

   c He ate his breakfast and left the table.

   d He dressed himself and went downstairs.

   e Michael got out of bed at eight o'clock.

4 a They walked about collecting moon rocks.

   b The rocket took off from the moon with a
      loud blast from its engines.

   c Two spacemen climbed out of the rocket.

   d The rocket landed safely on the moon.

   e The spacemen climbed back into their
      rocket.

Going to school

Lydia Henry and her brother Errol go to the same school. Lydia is one year older than Errol but she is shorter than he is. Everyone thinks she is his little sister.

Lydia and Errol go to Little River Primary School. Lydia is in Class 3 and Errol is in Class 2. The school is not far from their home but they have jobs to do every morning so they get up at six o'clock.

Errol fetches clean water from the spring near Little River. He helps Lydia to milk the goats. Then they cross the river and climb a little hill to get to school.

1   Who is taller, Lydia or Errol?

2   Who is older, Lydia or Errol?

3   Why does everyone think Lydia is Errol's little sister?

4   What is the name of their school?

5   When do they get up in the morning?

6   What does Errol do before he goes to school?

7   What does Lydia do before she goes to school?

8   Where do they walk to get to school?

Opposites: using un

tidy

untidy

We can give some words an opposite meaning by writing **un** before them.

Look at the words **tidy** and **untidy**, above the pictures.

A   Write the opposites of these words by using **un**.

1	lock	5	kind	9	known
2	paid	6	do	10	tie
3	well	7	screw	11	load
4	pack	8	wind	12	wrap

B   Choose any six of the words you have made and use them in sentences of your own.

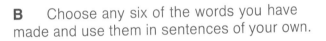

C   Write out these sentences, adding **un** to the words in bold type so as to give them an opposite meaning.

1   It did not take Norma long to **dress**.

2   The room was very **tidy**.

3   This water is **fit** for drinking.

4   What he said was **true**.

5   The injured man was **able** to walk.

6   Ian sat in a corner looking very **happy**.

7   They were **willing** to go.

8   The bridge was **safe** for traffic.

Opposites: change of words

tall

short

The words **tall** and **short** are **opposite** in meaning.

bad	good
big	small
cold	hot
early	late
empty	full
hard	soft
in	out
new	old
open	shut
strong	weak
tall	short
tame	wild
harmful	harmless

Learn the pairs of opposites in the list on the left, then put the right word in each space in the sentences below.

1 Mr. Henry bought a new car and sold the ___ one.

2 Fire is a ___ servant but a bad master.

3 I was late for school yesterday, but I was ___ today.

4 The lion is strong, but the mouse is ___.

5 There was hot and ___ water in the bathroom.

6 Some beds are hard; others are ___.

7 Mr. Gibbs was in, but Mrs. Gibbs was ___.

8 Paul is a tall boy, but his brother Mark is quite ___.

9 The shop is open on Saturday and ___ on Sunday.

10 Some snakes are harmful and some are ___.

Adding -ed to doing words

When we add **-ed** to **doing** words ending with **y** we change the **y** to **i**.

	try	marry
Change the **y** to **i**	tr**i**	marr**i**
Add on **-ed**	tr**ied**	marr**ied**

With these words the **y** is changed to **i** and **-d** only is added.

pay	lay	say
paid	laid	said

I tidy my bedroom.

I tidied my bedroom.

A Add **-ed** to each of these words. Remember to change the **y** to **i**.

1	dry	4	tidy	7	hurry
2	carry	5	cry	8	fry
3	copy	6	bury	9	empty

B Use the words you have made to fill the spaces.

1 I ___ to catch the train.

2 Mother ___ fish for our lunch.

3 Janet ___ when she fell off the wall.

4 Keith ___ the heavy basket all the way home.

5 The sun and the wind soon ___ the washing.

6 The children ___ the room after the party.

7 The dog ___ a bone in the garden.

8 Bill ___ the words in his notebook.

9 The men ___ the garbage into the truck.

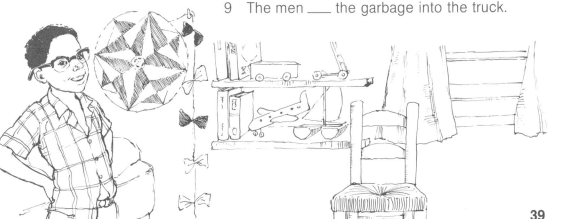

Two word games

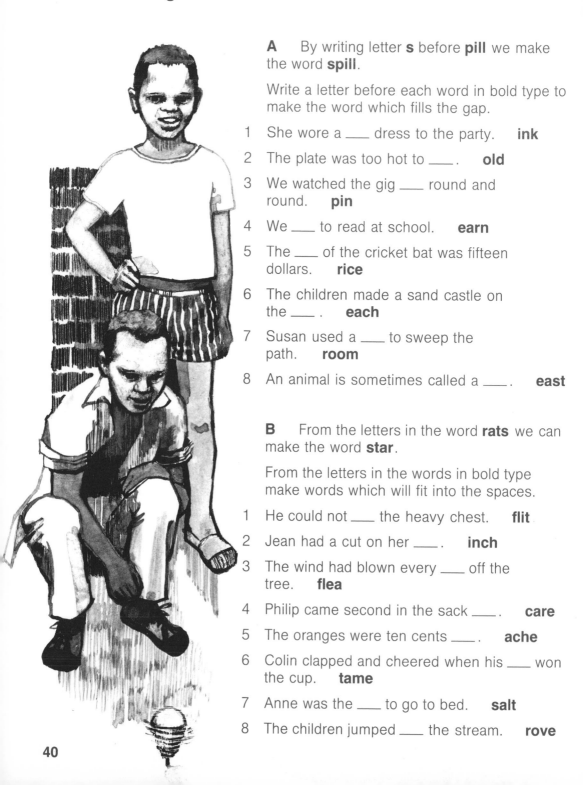

A   By writing letter **s** before **pill** we make the word **spill**.

Write a letter before each word in bold type to make the word which fills the gap.

1   She wore a ___ dress to the party.   **ink**

2   The plate was too hot to ___.   **old**

3   We watched the gig ___ round and round.   **pin**

4   We ___ to read at school.   **earn**

5   The ___ of the cricket bat was fifteen dollars.   **rice**

6   The children made a sand castle on the ___.   **each**

7   Susan used a ___ to sweep the path.   **room**

8   An animal is sometimes called a ___.   **east**

B   From the letters in the word **rats** we can make the word **star**.

From the letters in the words in bold type make words which will fit into the spaces.

1   He could not ___ the heavy chest.   **flit**

2   Jean had a cut on her ___.   **inch**

3   The wind had blown every ___ off the tree.   **flea**

4   Philip came second in the sack ___.   **care**

5   The oranges were ten cents ___.   **ache**

6   Colin clapped and cheered when his ___ won the cup.   **tame**

7   Anne was the ___ to go to bed.   **salt**

8   The children jumped ___ the stream.   **rove**

40

Using has and have

For **one** person or thing we use **has**.

For **more than one** person or thing we use **have**.

Always use **have** with **I** or **you**.

Our cat **has** kittens.
Uncle Selwyn **has** bought a new car.

The monkeys **have** long tails.
The children **have** gone to the circus.

I **have** a bad cold.
You **have** grown quite a lot.

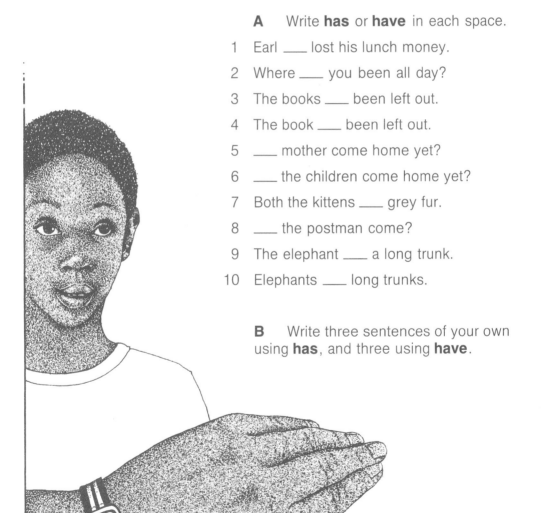

A   Write **has** or **have** in each space.

1   Earl ___ lost his lunch money.

2   Where ___ you been all day?

3   The books ___ been left out.

4   The book ___ been left out.

5   ___ mother come home yet?

6   ___ the children come home yet?

7   Both the kittens ___ grey fur.

8   ___ the postman come?

9   The elephant ___ a long trunk.

10   Elephants ___ long trunks.

B   Write three sentences of your own using **has**, and three using **have**.

The Storm

Thunder
rumbles
grumbles
tumbles
way up high

Lightning
flashes
splashes
crashes
through the air

Rainclouds
furry
hurry
scurry
through the sky

Raindrops
patter
spatter
clatter
everywhere

Pamela   Mordecai

1   Which words rhyme with rumbles?

2   Which words rhyme with flashes?

3   Write out the words that rhyme with furry.

4   Write out the words that rhyme with patter.

5   Do high and sky rhyme?

6   Do air and everywhere rhyme?

Martin and Pam

This is Martin

This is Pam

A   See how Martin is dressed.
Use the words in the list on the left to fill the spaces.

shirt
gloves
boots
trousers
cap

1   On his head Martin wears a ___ .

2   He wears a white short-sleeved ___ .

3   On his feet he wears cricket ___ .

4   He wears long white ___ .

5   On his hands Martin wears batting ___ .

B   See what Pam is wearing. Use the words in the list on the left to fill the spaces.

blouse
scarf
skirt
shoes
sash

1   Pam wears a white peasant ___ .

2   Round her waist she wears a ___ .

3   On her feet she wears ___ .

4   She wears a plaid gathered ___ .

5   Pam wears a ___ tied around her hair.

Write a few sentences telling how any boy or girl in your class is dressed.

Things we eat and drink

You may drink a **glass** of fruit juice if you are thirsty.

We can buy a **loaf** of bread at the shop.

Copy the words below and fill in the gaps. The words you need are in exercise B.

A

1   a bunch of ___

2   a loaf of ___

3   a bottle of ___

4   a bowl of ___

5   a tin of ___

6   a bar of ___

7   a jar of ___

8   a cup of ___

B   What are the missing words?

1   a ___ of sugar

2   a ___ of bread

3   a ___ of peanut butter

4   a ___ of tea

5   a ___ of beer

6   a ___ of bananas

7   a ___ of chocolate

8   a ___ of sardines

44

Rhymes

Pussy Cat, Pussy Cat, what have you seen?
I've been to London and seen the Queen.
Pussy Cat, Pussy Cat, what did you there?
I frightened a little mouse under her chair.

The words **seen** and **Queen** end with the same sound.

So do the words **there** and **chair**.

Words which end with the same sound are said to **rhyme**.

A   Write the two words that rhyme in each group below.

1	man	2	bed	3	same
	far		bee		take
	bat		leg		tale
	can		pen		cane
	tap		pet		sail
	wag		sea		race

4	team	5	fear	6	late
	seat		beat		laid
	lean		bear		wait
	leap		peel		pain
	seed		hair		sail
	meet		real		page

B   Here are twenty words. Write them as ten pairs of words which rhyme, like this:

trip   sore   hill
ship   four   fill

1	trip	8	peas	15	seal
2	sore	9	pull	16	card
3	hill	10	hard	17	full
4	down	11	brown	18	fill
5	line	12	fine	19	bees
6	peel	13	ship	20	harm
7	four	14	farm		

Using did and done

Pam **did** all the work.

Pam **has done** all the work.

(**has** helps the word **done**)

All the work **was done** by Pam.

(**was** helps the word **done**)

The word **did** does not need a helping word.

The word **done** always has a helping word:

has done
have done
is done
are done
was done
were done
had done

A   Use **did** or **done** to fill each space.

1   I ___

2   You have ___

3   It was ___

4   He ___

5   You ___

6   He has ___

7   We ___

8   They are ___

9   She ___

10 We had ___

B   Fill each space with **did** or **done**.

1   Rani ___ her best to finish her homework.

2   We have ___ some good work today.

3   The soldier ___ his duty.

4   This drawing was ___ by Robert.

5   Robert ___ this drawing himself.

6   The gardener has ___ the lawns.

7   When the cakes are ___ you may have one.

8   When I was ill Jean ___ the cooking.

9   Leonie ___ some gardening and then she went out.

10 After Leonie had ___ some gardening she went out.

Words with more than one meaning

Some words have more than one meaning.

Don't **drop** that plate!

There is not a **drop** of milk left.

back
band
calf
lean
left
mine
post
stick
suit

Use the words in the list on the left to fill these spaces. The same word must be used for both sentences in each pair.

1   I hurt my ___ when I fell from the tree?
    I will be ___ in half an hour.

2   A ___ is a young cow.
    The back of the leg below the knee is called the ___ .

3   A new ___ was put up to hold the clothes line.
    Would you like me to ___ your letter?

4   Please don't ___ against the glass door.
    This beef is very ___ .

5   Companies ___ bauxite in Jamaica and Guyana.
    Your bat is much better than ___ .

6   The ___ played a lively tune.
    The man had a ___ of black ribbon around his hat.

7   George writes with his ___ hand.
    There are only two avocado pears ___ in the dish.

8   Will you ___ a stamp on this envelope?
    He used a short ___ to make a fishing rod.

9   Brian wore his new blue ___ to the wedding.
    Maureen's new dress does not ___ her at all.

Ice-cream in Rio Claro

Lydia and Errol can tell when Uncle Harold is coming to visit. They hear the sound of his old motorcycle as it climbs the hill to their house. Whenever he visits them, the children get a special treat.

First he hugs and kisses them. Then he asks, "Who wants to come with me to Rio Claro for some ice-cream?"

Lydia and Errol love to ride on Uncle Harold's motorcycle. It has a little sidecar that Lydia sits in. Errol sits behind Uncle Harold and holds on tightly around his waist.

Soon they are in Rio Claro at Mrs. Hill's ice-cream parlour. There are so many flavours of ice-cream to choose from: mango, coconut, rum and raisin, vanilla, coffee, chocolate and many more. Uncle Harold lets the children have three scoops each. Lydia has a scoop of coconut, a scoop of coffee and a scoop of vanilla. Errol has three scoops of chocolate. Uncle Harold just smiles and watches them eat.

1 How can the children tell when Uncle Harold is coming to visit?

2 What is the special treat which they get when Uncle Harold visits?

3 Where does Errol sit on Uncle Harold's motorbike?

4 Where does Lydia sit?

5 Why does Errol hold on tightly around Uncle Harold's waist?

6 What are some of the flavours at Mrs. Hill's ice-cream parlour?

7 Which are the flavours that Lydia likes?

8 Which flavour does Errol like?

Same sound – different meaning

Some words have the same sound as other words, but they are different in spelling and in meaning.

Look at these four pairs of words.

by	He was standing **by** the door.
buy	I will **buy** you a bar of chocolate.
made	The toy was **made** in Trinidad.
maid	The **maid** dusted the chairs.
some	You can't have all the sweets but you may have **some**.
sum	The **sum** of one and one is two.
tale	A **tale** is a story.
tail	The mongoose has a long **tail**.

Choose the right word from the pair above to fill each space.

1 **some**   **sum**
   I can't work this ___ .

2 **tale**   **tail**
   Uncle Harold read a fairy ___ to Lydia.

3 **by**   **buy**
   I am going to ___ some sweets.

4 **some**   **sum**
   ___ people are kind but others are not.

5 **made**   **maid**
   Kay ___ a dress for herself.

6 **tale**   **tail**
   Our dog wags his ___ when he is happy.

7 **by**   **buy**
   The family went to Venezuela ___ boat.

8 **made**   **maid**
   The new ___ tidied the bedrooms in the hotel.

People who work

A   Use the words in the list to name each person. Number your words from 1 to 8 as in the pictures.

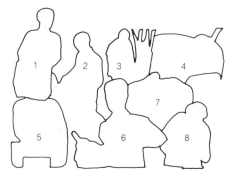

baker	miner
butcher	pilot
doctor	postman
farmer	shoemaker
garbageman	barber
grocer	

B   Who am I?

1 I bring letters and parcels to your home.

2 You buy meat from me.

3 I try to cure you when you are ill.

4 I mend your shoes and boots.

5 I dig gold and diamonds from the earth.

6 You come to me for your haircut.

7 I fly aeroplanes all over the world.

8 I make bread, buns and cakes.

9 I collect rubbish from your house.

10 I sell bacon, cheese, flour, cocoa, sugar and other things.

The not words

We sometimes join **not** to another word.

When we do this we leave out the **o** in **not** and write **'** in its place

Examples

is not	isn't
was not	wasn't
does not	doesn't
has not	hasn't
are not	aren't
were not	weren't
do not	don't
have not	haven't

Remember that the **'** must go where the **o** was.

A   Join each pair of words together.

1   does not
2   were not
3   has not
4   is not
5   have not
6   was not
7   do not
8   are not

B   Write these sentences, using one word in place of the two words in bold type in each line.

1   A donkey **does not** make the same noise as a horse.
2   The twins **were not** in school today.
3   Derek **has not** gone to school yet.
4   This milk **is not** fresh.
5   **Was not** that a dainty dish to set before the king?
6   Some children **do not** have lunch at school.
7   We **have not** had the treat you promised us.
8   These oranges **are not** very sweet.

Using do and does

We use **does** when we speak of **one person or thing**.

We use **do** when we speak of **more than one**.

Always use **do** with **you**, even for one person.

Always use **do** with **I**.

One	More than one
I do	we do
you do	you do
he, she, it does	they do

A   Fill each space with **do** or **does**.

1   Martin ___ his exercises every morning.

2   Many people ___ exercises to keep fit.

3   I hope you ___ well in the test.

4   Our Alsatian ___ make a good watchdog.

5   Susan and I ___ our homework together.

6   Henry ___ his best to keep the garden tidy.

B   **Don't** and **doesn't** follow the same rules.

Write **don't** or **doesn't** in each space.

1   We ___ go to bed very early on weekends.

2   The shop ___ close till six o'clock.

3   Jane ___ like washing up.

4   You will miss the bus if you ___ hurry.

5   I ___ go to the pictures very often.

6   Colin ___ want any breakfast this morning.

Capital letters

Capital letters are used –

1   to begin a sentence

2   for the names of people and pets

3   for the names of places, rivers, mountains and so on

4   for the names of the days of the week and months of the year

A   There are **fourteen words** in this list which should begin with a capital letter. Write them in the order in which they come.

fine	france	monday
kingston	shoes	demerara
plate	columbus	jones
george	antigua	table
bread	banana	arthur
friday	betty	chest
thomson	april	paper
apple	chicken	july

B   Write these sentences in your book. Use **capital letters** where they are needed.

1   did you know that i was seven last sunday?

2   linda and charles live on church street.

3   roy goes to barbados every christmas.

4   i take my dog silas for a walk every day.

5   jack and jill went up the hill.

6   mr. singh has a cow named daisy.

7   we shall be moving to port-of-spain next tuesday.

8   the blue mountains are the highest mountains in jamaica.

Children at play

David   Jill

Betty   Yvonne   Lloyd   Roger

Look at these children at play. Use the
words from the list on the left to finish each
sentence below.

1 David is on roller ___ .

2 He is going very ___ .

3 Betty and Yvonne are having a ___ race.

4 Roger and Lloyd are playing ___ .

branch
fast
holding
marbles
skates
skipping
swing
thick

5 Lloyd is ___ a marble in his right hand.

6 Jill is on the ___ .

7 The swing hangs from a ___ of the tree.

8 The trunk of the tree is very ___ .

54

Joining words

Some words are made by joining two words together.

arm + chair = armchair

A   The names of things you see in the pictures are made in this way. Copy them from the list on the left.

birdcage   bookshelf
cupboard   tablecloth
eggcup   teapot
flowerpot   dustbin

B   Join the two words in bold type in each sentence to make one word, starting with the second word.

Example   1   keyhole

1   A **hole** in the door for the **key**.

2   A **mill** which is worked by the **wind**.

3   The land at the **side** of the **sea**.

4   A **worm** which spins **silk** threads.

5   A **coat** which is worn in the **rain**.

6   A **bag** carried in the **hand**.

7   The **sty** in which a **pig** is kept.

8   A **room** for a **bed**.

9   A **ball** game which is played with the **foot**.

10   The **bell** on a **door**.

Doing words: past time

We do not always add **-ed** to doing words to show **past time**.

	Now	Past
	Today I **fly**.	Yesterday I **flew**.
	Today I **come**.	Last week I **came**.

Learn the words in the list, then do the exercises.

Present	Past
bite	bit
break	broke
come	came
creep	crept
do	did
draw	drew
drink	drank
fall	fell
fly	flew
give	gave
hide	hid
wear	wore

A   Copy these columns. Fill the blanks.

Present Past

Present	Past		Present	Past
1 draw	___	7	___	broke
2 drink	___	8	___	hid
3 bite	___	9	___	crept
4 fly	___	10	do	___
5 ___	came	11	___	fell
6 ___	wore	12	give	___

B   Put the right word in each space.

1 Ronald ___ the ball in the drawer.   **hide**

2 Mrs. Miller ___ Errol a bun.   **give**

3 The bird ___ away when we got near.   **fly**

4 A big dog ___ Susan on the leg.   **bite**

5 Who ___ this lovely picture?   **draw**

6 The football ___ the window.   **break**

7 Philip ___ all his homework.   **do**

8 Sheila ___ her new shoes yesterday.
wear

Opposites: change of word

Learn this list of opposites then answer the questions.

begin	finish
bottom	top
clean	dirty
down	up
dry	wet
fresh	stale
give	take
high	low
over	under
pretty	ugly
right	wrong
thick, fat	thin

A   Write the opposites of these words.

1	ugly	7	down
2	thin	8	bottom
3	wrong	9	dirty
4	under	10	finish
5	stale	11	dry
6	take	12	high

B   Copy these sentences. In each space write the opposite of the word in bold type.

1 Neville rode **up** the lane, then ___ again.

2 The show will **begin** at 7 o'clock and ___ at 9 o'clock.

3 The **clean** plates were put away and the ___ ones were put in the sink.

4 The ___ of the pole was thicker than the **top**.

5 Three sums were **right** and one was ___ .

6 The bakery had no **fresh** loaves, only ___ ones.

7 Please **take** this juice away and ___ me some milk.

8 Aston jumped **over** the bar. David ducked ___ it.

9 Barry likes **thick** slices of bread. Jean only eats ___ slices.

10 Joy looks **pretty** when she smiles but ___ when she frowns.

57

Same sound – different meaning

Look at the four pairs of words below.

The words in each pair have the same sound but are different in spelling and meaning.

not	Mrs. Young was **not** at home.
knot	There was a **knot** in the rope.
new	The **new** car is faster than the old one.
knew	Richard **knew** all the songs the class sang.
sea	Several ships were sailing on the **sea**.
see	We **see** with our eyes.
our	**Our** things are the things that belong to us.
hour	There are sixty minutes in an **hour**.

Fill each space with the right word.

1 Henry wore his ___ shirt to school.

2 The boat was wrecked in the stormy ___ .

3 I did ___ eat the apple because it was bad.

4 Jenny ___ her tables well.

5 We put ___ books into the desks.

6 From the top of the tower we could ___ the ___ .

7 James could ___ untie the ___ in his shoelace.

8 The schoolchildren get an ___ for lunch.

Collections

Look at the words used for each collection below.

We call a number of sheep together a **flock**.

1   a box of ___

3   a bunch of ___

5   a pack of ___

7   a herd of ___

A   Use the pictures to help you fill in the gaps.

2   a crowd of ___

4   a clump of ___

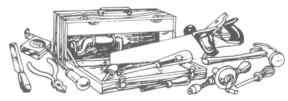

6   a set of ___

8   a flock of ___

B   What are the missing words?

1   a ___ of flowers   5   a ___ of sheep

2   a ___ of elephants   6   a ___ of trees

3   a ___ of cards   7   a ___ of chocolates

4   a ___ of people   8   a ___ of tools

Down by the river

On Saturday mornings Errol and Lydia go down by the river. Errol looks for river shrimp under the rocks. Lydia tries to swim across a little pool in the river. Errol can swim well and sometimes he helps Lydia. He shows her how to move her arms and legs.

When Lydia is tired she sits against one of the big rocks in the river and lets the water run down her back and splash over her head and arms. "It's fun," she tells Errol. "It's like a big shower."

Sometimes Errol makes a fishing rod from a long stick and twine and a bent pin. He uses a worm as bait. Then he sits very still on a rock and waits. He gets mad at Lydia if she splashes in the water or makes a noise. "But you never catch any fish," Lydia says. Then he really gets vexed and splashes her all over with water.

Write down the words in list **a**. Next to each write the word or phrase from list **b** which could replace it in the passage without changing the meaning, e.g. **rod** ... pole.

a	b
rod	angry
twine	pole
bait	string
vexed	food to catch fish

1 What do Lydia and Errol do on Saturday mornings?

2 What does Errol do down by the river?

3 What does Lydia do?

4 How does Errol help Lydia?

5 What does Lydia do when she is tired?

6 What does Errol make his fishing rod from?

7 What does he use for bait?

8 What makes Errol get angry with Lydia?

Showing ownership

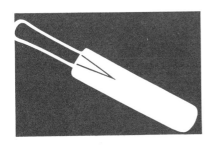

This is Errol's bat.

The **'s** shows that Errol **owns** the bat.

Look at these pictures.

See who **owns** each thing.

Write **'s** after each child's name to finish the exercise. The first is done for you.

1 Errol

2 Sarah

3 Lydia

4 Peter

5 Alan

6 Janet

7 David

8 Pam

Copy these in your book.

1	Errol's bat	5	___ car
2	___ teddy bear	6	___ pram
3	___ ball	7	___ scooter
4	___ gig	8	___ cat

Groups

A petunia is a **flower**.   A cat is an **animal**.   An owl is a **bird**.   A palm is a **tree**.

A   Draw four columns in your book like these. Then put the words below in their proper places.

Animals	Birds	Trees	Flowers
cedar	nightingale	poui	fir
parrot	pig	cow	rose
hibiscus	lily	flamingo	goat
sheep	crow	marigold	mahogany
macaw	orchid	mahoe	donkey

B   Draw these four columns in your book. Put the words in their proper places.

Tools	Clothes	Furniture	Colours
table	coat	yellow	axe
spanner	hammer	shorts	wardrobe
green	shirt	skirt	saw
chair	sofa	blue	brown
cutlass	red	tie	bed

Similar words

Some words mean much the same as other words:

A **large** house
A **big** house

The words **large** and **big** are **similar**, or **alike**, in meaning.

Learn these similar words, then do the exercises.

creep	crawl
finish	end
halt	stop
large	big
present	gift
speak	talk
start	begin
stout	fat
tear	rip
tug	pull

A In place of each word in bold type write a word which has a **similar** meaning.

1 I **start** work at eight o'clock.

2 Snakes **creep** along the ground.

3 Carl gave Diana's hair a playful **tug**.

4 A **large** crowd saw a fine game.

5 They do not **speak** to each other now.

6 Cars must **halt** at the crossroads.

7 The cook was a **stout** person.

8 There is a **tear** in my dress.

9 Carol had a lovely **present** from her aunt.

10 Our holiday will **finish** next Sunday.

B For each word below write one which is similar in meaning.

1 big

2 talk

3 end

4 pull

5 gift

6 crawl

7 stop

8 begin

9 rip

10 fat

Describing words

The rabbit has **long** ears.

The word **long** tells **what kind** of ears the rabbit has.

Because it **describes** the ears, we call it a **describing** word.

A   Choose one of the words in the list on the left to describe each of the things below.

fast
gold
tasty
kind
shady
ripe
playful
silk
blazing
rough

1   a ___ dog   6   a ___ fire

2   a ___ tree   7   a ___ meal

3   a ___ sea   8   a ___ car

4   a ___ ring   9   a ___ friend

5   a ___ sari   10   a ___ mango

B   Now use the best describing word you can think of for each of these words.

1   a ___ boy   5   a ___ field

2   a ___ wind   6   a ___ flower

3   a ___ dress   7   a ___ kitten

4   a ___ policeman   8   a ___ orange

C   Fill each gap with a suitable naming word.

1   a lovely ___   5   a quiet ___

2   a naughty ___   6   a clean ___

3   a sunny ___   7   a clever ___

4   a wide ___   8   a wild ___

Same sound – different meaning

Look at the four pairs of words below.

The words in each pair have the same sound but are different in spelling and meaning.

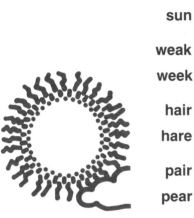

son — Mr. Weekes has one **son** and one daughter.

sun — The **sun** rises in the east and sets in the west.

weak — The sick man was too **weak** to get up.

week — There are seven days in a **week**.

hair — **Hair** grows on your head.

hare — A **hare** is an animal very much like a rabbit.

pair — A **pair** is a set of two, like a pair of shoes.

pear — An avocado **pear** has a large seed in the middle.

Fill each space with the right word.

1 Father bought a new ___ of shoes.

2 The heat of the ___ makes plants grow.

3 The woman had black curly ___.

4 The school was closed for a ___.

5 This ___ is not quite ripe.

6 The ___ has long ears and a short tail.

7 Mary was quite ___ after her long illness.

8 The farmer told his ___ to fetch a cutlass.

Carnival

On the last days before Ash Wednesday everyone in Little River takes part in Carnival. Bands of people in bright costumes dance through the streets. They move to the sound of steel band music. The steel pans are on wheels and people push them through the streets. The pan men play all the new calypsoes and road marches.

The children in Little River have their own costume bands. Last year, Lydia and Errol played in a sailor band. This year they are dressing up as pirates. They hope their band will win the prize for the best costumes.

The children have their own calypso competition too. They have to make up the words and the melodies all by themselves. It is great fun.

Write down the words in list **a**. Next to each write the word or phrase from list **b** which could replace it in the passage without changing the meaning.

a	b
bands	tunes
steel pans	men who play on steel drums
pan men	contest
competition	steel drums
melodies	groups

1 Everyone in Little ____ takes part in ____ .
2 Carnival is on the ____ few ____ before Ash ____ .
3 ____ of people in ____ costumes ____ through the streets.
4 They ____ to the sound of ____ band ____ .
5 Last ____ Lydia and Errol ____ in a ____ band.
6 ____ year they are ____ up as ____ .
7 They ____ their band will ____ the prize for the ____ ____ .
8 The ____ have their own ____ competition.
9 They ____ up the ____ and ____ all by ____ .
10 It is ____ ____ .

Fun with words

Can you make these words from the word
holiday?

1 o – –   aged
2 o – –   you pour it on troubled waters
3 l – –   boy
4 l – –   cover
5 h – –   dried grass
6 l – –   the hens do this to the eggs
7 h – –   made sure no one could see you.
8 h – – –   grasp
9 d – –   opposite of night
10 l – – –   something you carry

Riddle me ree

This is a rhyming riddle. The answer has the
same sound as the last word in one of the
lines. Can you guess the answer?

There are times when
If I touch you
I'm so hot
I'll make you scream
But you cannot ever touch me –
Can you guess what I am?

Rhymes

A   Write this poem in your book.
Use the words in the list on the left to fill the spaces.

Sleep

bed	girls
feet	night
sack	still
back	alight
will	street
said	curls

In the dark and lonely ___ ,
When the stars are all ___ ,
Sleep comes creeping up the ___
With her naked, silent ___ ,
Carrying upon her ___ ,
Dreams of all kinds in a ___ ;
Though the doors are bolted, ___
She can enter where she ___ ,
And she lingers, it is ___ ,
Longest by the children's ___ ;
Smooths their pillows, strokes their ___ ,
Happy little boys and ___ !

B   Write one word which rhymes with each pair below. For the first word you could choose from:

fed   led   red   shed   dead   head   bread   tread

1   bed   said ___   4   still   will ___

2   feet   street ___   5   night   bite ___

3   back   sack ___   6   try   lie ___

Using is and his/Using as and has

Tom **is** tall, Teddy and Tyrone **are** not.

Hugh lost **his** book. **His** means **belonging to him**.

A   Use **is** or **his** to fill each space.

1   This book ___ really funny.

2   Father cut ___ finger with a sharp knife.

3   Billy often gives ___ dog a bone.

4   The dog ___ an alsatian.

5   ___ uncle ___ a farmer.

6   When ___ Roy going to eat ___ banana?

7   Ann ___ seven, but David ___ only five.

8   Noel helps both ___ father and ___ mother.

As I turned I slipped. It was **as** cold **as** ice.

Eric **has** a football. **Has** means **owns**.

Peter **has** come back. He **has** grown very tall.

B   Use **as** or **has** to fill each space.

1   Richard ___ a new bat.

2   June is ___ tall ___ Helen.

3   The fisherman whistled ___ he mended his net.

4   Where ___ Karen put the sweets?

5   He knocked his head ___ he bent down.

6   ___ anybody seen my book?

7   I think Linda ___ grown ___ tall ___ Jane.

8   Father ___ a meal ___ soon ___ he comes home.

69

Jumbled sentences

The words in this sentence are not in their right order.

a has tail monkey The long

This sentence has the words in their right order.

The monkey has a long tail.

Put the words in these sentences in their correct order.

The capital letter shows which word comes first.

Put a full stop at the end of each sentence.

1 fighting ram goats are two The

2 climbing girl is a tree The

3 grass is The cow some eating

4 very donkey A ears long has

5 a horse is cart The pulling

6 is boy a The bicycle riding

Telling the time

The **little hand** of a clock or watch is called the **hour hand**. The little hand says the hour.

The **big hand** is called the **minute hand**.

When the big hand points to **12**, it says **o'clock**.

This is three o'clock.

This is nine o'clock.

Write these times.

When the big hand points to **6** it says **half past**.

This is half past three.

This is half past nine.

Write these times.

When the big hand points to **3** it says **quarter past**.

This is quarter past three.

This is quarter past nine.

Write these times.

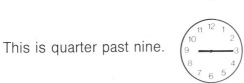

In the garden

On Saturday afternoons Sonia and Tony Khan work in the garden with their parents. Sonia works with her mother in the vegetable garden. She digs up weeds with a small fork and puts them in the wheelbarrow. Mrs. Khan prepares the soil for planting seeds. The two children help her to reap the vegetables that are ready for market.

Mr. Khan cuts the lawn. Tony's job is to rake the grass into small heaps. He rakes up the dead leaves too. He puts the grass and leaves into the barrow. The children take turns wheeling the barrow down to the bottom of the garden. They throw the grass and dead leaves into one heap and the weeds into another.

When the work is finished, Mr. Khan sets fire to the weeds. He covers the heap of dead leaves and grass with some earth. When the grass and leaves rot, they will help to make the soil in the garden rich.

Write down the words in list **a**. Next to each write the word or phrase from list **b** which could replace it in the passage without changing the meaning

a	**b**
prepares	earth
soil	over, done
reap	makes ready
heaps	gather up
finished	piles

1 What do Sonia and Tony do on Saturday afternoons?

2 Where does Sonia work?

3 What does she do?

4 Who prepares the soil for planting seeds?

5 What do the two children help Mrs. Khan to do?

6 What does Mr. Khan do?

7 Who wheels the barrow to the bottom of the garden?

8 What happens to the heap of weeds?

9 What will the grass and dead leaves help to do when they rot?

A day in Joy's life

Copy each sentence in your book.
Fill in the time shown by each clock.

1 Joy woke at .... 2 She got up at ....

3 Joy was dressed by ..... 4 She had breakfast at ....

5 Joy got to school at ...... 6 She went out for lunch at ....

7 Joy left school at .... 8 She had dinner at ....

Where they live

Learn the names of the homes of these creatures.

Creature	Home
bee	hive
bird	nest
dog	kennel
horse	stable
crab	hole
pig	sty
chicken	coop
spider	web
parrot	cage

Write the missing words.

1 A crab lives in a ___ .

2 A ___ is the home of a spider.

3 The horse lives in a ___ . 4 A ___ is a dog's home. 5 Bees live in a ___ .

6 A pig lives in a ___ . 7 Chickens live in a ___ . 8 A parrot usually lives in a ___ .

74

Describing words

A Use the words in the list on the left to describe the things below.

bright
fresh
chubby
wooden
sharp
china
juicy
heavy

1 a ___ parcel
2 a ___ egg
3 a ___ star
4 a ___ teapot
5 a ___ knife
6 a ___ baby
7 a ___ orange
8 a ___ stool

B From the words in the list on the left choose the one which will best fit each line.

Example
1 The washing on the line is **clean**.
   So the word **clean** fits line 1.

fine
stale
rich
clean
new
tidy
ripe
quiet

1 The washing on the line is ___ .

2 A pear which is ready for eating is ___ .

3 A person who has a lot of money is ___ .

4 A child who makes no noise is ___ .

5 A day when there is no rain is ___ .

6 Bread which was baked a week ago is ___ .

7 A dress which has never been worn is ___ .

8 A room in which nothing is out of place is ___ .

Hidden words

A   Use a word of two letters to fill the gap in each of these sentences.

Example
1   At the seaside the children played in the s _ _ d.

Answer   s**an**d

1   At the seaside the children played in the s _ _ d.

2   The box was too heavy for Tom to l _ _ t.

3   The man struck a m _ _ ch to light his pipe.

4   Hot weather makes the butter very s _ _ t.

5   He did not have a w _ _ k of sleep last night.

6   Tony's pants were d _ _ p after the rain.

7   Martin caught a big f _ _ h with his new rod.

8   Six ducks were swimming on the p _ _ d.

9   Paul came l _ _ t in the race.

10   There were all s _ _ ts of toys in the shop.

B   A word of three letters is hidden in each of the words in bold type. Find the ten words.

1   **grate**
an animal

2   **harmful**
part of the body

3   **plantain**
a small insect

4   **scarf**
we travel in it

5   **shears**
we listen with them

6   **scowl**
a big animal

7   **champion**
something to eat

8   **steal**
something to drink

9   **beggar**
we get it from a hen

10   **slipper**
a part of your mouth

Matching parts of sentences

Here you see two parts of a sentence.

Jane went to bed early   because she was so tired.

Each sentence below is in two parts, but the parts have become mixed up.

Write the first part of each sentence then add on the part which fits it.

1   The leaves were falling   a very long neck.

2   Tony and Sheila   is called a lamb.

3   The cat lapped up   go to the seaside.

4   Our baby likes   are brother and sister.

5   The turtle has   is called a stable.

6   A baby sheep   from the trees.

7   People often catch cold   a hard shell on its back.

8   A giraffe has   all the milk in the dish.

9   The home of a horse   to play with his rattle.

10   On weekends many people   in very wet weather.

Going to market

When school is on holiday, Lydia and Errol go to market with their mother. The market is in Charlestown. Charlestown is twenty kilometres from Little River, so they have to take a bus.

Mrs. Henry takes cabbages, carrots and peas to sell in the market. She packs them carefully in big bags. She stuffs dried leaves into the bags so that the cabbages and carrots will not be damaged on their way to market.

The bus is an old bus that leans to one side. Someone lifts Mrs. Henry's bags on top of the bus and ties them on tightly. Then Mrs. Henry and the children get in and the bus drives off.

The bus goes very fast. The hills and rivers and fields of cane seem to race past. Errol does not like to go so fast but Lydia loves it. "It's like being on an aeroplane", she says.

Write down the words in list **a**. Next to each write the word or phrase from list **b** which could replace it in the passage without changing the meaning.

a	b
packs	taking great care
carefully	puts
stuffs	rush
damaged	pushes
race	harmed, hurt

1 When do Lydia and Errol go to market with their mother?

2 Where is the market?

3 Why do they have to take a bus to market?

4 What does Mrs. Henry take to sell in the market?

5 Why does she stuff dried leaves in the bags of carrots and cabbages?

6 Where are the bags of vegetables put?

7 What does the bus look like?

8 Why do the hills and rivers and fields of cane seem to fly past?

9 Why does Lydia like the bus to go fast?

Rhymes

A   In each group below write four words which rhyme with the word in bold type. The first letter of each new word is given.

1 **bat**
   h _ _
   m _ _
   c _ _
   f _ _

2 **cap**
   l _ _
   t _ _
   m _ _
   r _ _

3 **din**
   f _ _
   w _ _
   p _ _
   b _ _

4 **rut**
   c _ _
   n _ _
   b _ _
   h _ _

5 **best**
   v _ _ _
   n _ _ _
   r _ _ _
   w _ _ _

6 **lash**
   d _ _ _
   m _ _ _
   c _ _ _
   s _ _ _

7 **tent**
   b _ _ _
   s _ _ _
   l _ _ _
   r _ _ _

8 **meat**
   s _ _ _
   h _ _ _
   b _ _ _
   n _ _ _

9 **lack**
   p _ _ _
   s _ _ _
   r _ _ _
   b _ _ _

B   Use a word which rhymes with **came** to fill the space in each sentence.

1 The horse was _ _ _ _ and could not run in the race.

2 The dog's _ _ _ _ was Bimbo.

3 Cricket is the _ _ _ _ I like best.

4 The candle _ _ _ _ _ is yellow.

5 The twins wear the _ _ _ _ kinds of clothes.

6 The keeper stroked the lion cub which was quite _ _ _ _ .

7 The _ _ _ _ _ of the picture was made of wood.

Describing words: adding -er and -est

long

longer

longest

When we add **-er** or **-est** to a word ending with **e**, we drop the **e**.

wide

wider

widest

A   Add **-er** or **-est** to the words in bold type to fill the spaces.

1   Philip is much ___ than Derek.   **tall**

2   The church is the ___ building in town. **high**

3   Carol has the ___ writing in the class.   **neat**

4   At carnival on J'ouvert morning we wear the ___ clothes we have.   **warm**

5   I will write you a ___ letter next time.   **long**

6   This knife is ___ than yours.   **sharp**

B

Add **-er** or **est** to the words in bold type to fill the gaps.

1   The weather is much ___ today.   **fine**

2   This is the ___ jam I have ever tasted.   **nice**

3   The mango was ___ than the banana.   **ripe**

4   The old lion was the ___ of the lot.   **tame**

5   King Solomon was the ___ of all men.   **wise**

6   Your package is ___ than mine.   **large**

Beginning and ending sentences

A   Here are the beginnings of eight sentences. Finish each sentence yourself. Write them in your book.

1   At night the fireflies ....

2   The car was badly damaged ....

3   At the end of our street ....

4   When tea was over ....

5   The braying of the donkey ....

6   Mother sent for the doctor ....

7   Jane fed the puppy ....

8   The noise of the planes ....

B   Here are the endings of eight sentences. Write the first part of each in your own words.

1   .... so he went to bed.

2   .... and closed the door after him.

3   .... because of the heavy rain.

4   .... many trees were blown down.

5   ....but could not do it.

6   ....and put it in her purse.

7   ....when her kitten got lost.

8   ....and cut his knee.

Similar words

Some words mean much the same as other words.

A **wealthy** man
A **rich** man

The words **wealthy** and **rich** are **similar**, or **alike**, in meaning.

Learn these similar words, then do the exercises.

assist	help
broad	wide
correct	right
dwelling	home
farewell	goodbye
fast	quickly
raise	lift
repair	mend
reply	answer
wealthy	rich

A   In place of each word in bold type, write a word which has a similar meaning.

1   The main street was very **broad**.

2   He ran as **fast** as he could.

3   Colin could hardly **raise** his arm.

4   The cobbler will **repair** my shoes today.

5   Will you **assist** me with my sums?

6   The factory owner is a very **wealthy** man.

7   William had all his sums **correct**.

8   The **reply** to the question was very short.

9   The fisherman's **dwelling** was a small cottage.

10   The sailor said **farewell** to his wife.

B   For each word below write one which is similar in meaning.

1   home   5   help

2   goodbye   6   answer

3   lift   7   mend

4   rich   8   wide

Joining sentences using and

Read these two sentences.

John is tall.
John is strong.

We can join these
sentences by using **and**.

John is tall **and** and strong.
(This is a short way of saying John is tall
and John is strong.)

Here are more joined
sentences.

Mary put her toys away.
She went to bed.

Mary put her toys away **and** went to bed.

Use **and** to join each pair of sentences
below.

1   Our goat is black.
    Our goat has two kids.

2   The room was clean.
    The room was tidy.

3   Grandpa sat in the rocking chair.
    He fell fast asleep.

4   The day was fine.
    The day was warm.

5   I gave the grocer sixty cents.
    I got ten cents change.

6   The rice farmer floods the fields.
    He sows the seedlings.

7   We went to the botanical gardens.
    We played ball.

8   The nurse took my temperature.
    The nurse took my pulse.

9   Roy had his breakfast.
    Roy went to school.

I saw a ship a-sailing

I saw a ship a-sailing,
  A-sailing on the sea;
And it was deeply laden
  With pretty things for me.

There were raisins in the cabin
  And almonds in the hold;
The sails were made of satin,
  And the mast was made of gold.

The four and twenty sailors
  Who stood upon the decks
Were four and twenty white mice
  With rings about their necks.

The captain was a fine plump duck
  With a jacket on his back,
And when the fairy ship set sail
  The captain he said "Quack!"

1 Where were the raisins?

2 What were the sails made of?

3 What part of the ship was made of gold?

4 How many sailors stood on the decks?

5 Who were the sailors?

6 Who was the captain?

7 What did he have on his back?

8 What did the captain say when the ship set sail?

Things which are alike

When something is very **heavy** we say it is as **heavy** as **lead**.

This is because lead is a very, very heavy metal.

Learn the sayings in this list, then answer the questions below.

as cold as ice

as good as gold

as heavy as lead

as light as a feather

as quiet as a mouse

as slow as a snail

as sweet as sugar

as thin as a rake

as old as the hills

as hot as fire

A

1 as cold as ___
2 as hot as ___
3 as good as ___
4 as old as ___
5 as thin as a ___
6 as heavy as ___
7 as light as a ___
8 as sweet as ___
9 as quiet as a ___
10 as slow as a ___

B   Use the right word to finish each sentence.

1 That joke is as ___ as the hills.
2 The grapes were as ___ as sugar.
3 David was as ___ as gold in school.
4 The tea was as ___ as ice.
5 Jean's forehead was as ___ as fire.
6 The errand boy was as ___ as a snail.
7 This box is as ___ as a feather.
8 After his illness he was as ___ as a rake.

THE
QUIET
MOUSE

Describing words: adding -er and -est

When we add **-er** or **-est** to some words we **double the last letter**.

big   bigger   biggest

When we add **-er** or **-est** to words ending with **y** we change the **y** to **i**.

easy   easier   easiest

A

Add **-er** or **-est** to the words in bold type to fill the spaces.

1 This is the ___ day for years.   **hot**

2 Barbados is ___ than Antigua.   **flat**

3 Friday was the ___ day of the week.   **wet**

4 He picked the ___ slice of cake on the plate.   **thin**

5 The clown's nose was ___ than a cherry.   **red**

6 It was the ___ day of his life.   **sad**

B

1 John is the ___ boy in the whole world.   **happy**

2 Martin seems to be ___ than his brother.   **lazy**

3 The orchid is a ___ flower than the rose.   **pretty**

4 Her bedroom is the ___ room in the house.   **tidy**

5 The boys are ___ than the girls.   **noisy**

6 Christmas is the ___ time of year.   **merry**

Joining sentences using but

Read these two sentences.

We can join these sentences by using **but**.

See how these other sentences are joined.

Carol dropped her clock.
It did not break.

Carol dropped her clock **but** it did not break.

Paul fell down.
He did not cry.

Paul fell down **but** he did not cry.

The dog chased a mongoose.
He did not catch it.

The dog chased a mongoose **but** he did not catch it.

Use **but** to join each pair of sentences below.

1 Jill looked for her book.
   She could not find it.

2 We hoped to go out.
   It was too wet.

3 Easton fell off his scooter.
   He did not hurt himself.

4 The postman knocked at the gate.
   He could not get an answer.

5 They hurried to the airport.
   The plane had gone.

6 Sandra felt ill.
   She did not want to stay in bed.

7 Ann wanted a chocolate.
   The box was empty.

8 I longed for some ice-cream.
   I had no money.

9 We went into the playground.
   We did not stay long.

Using saw and seen

William **saw** a flamingo.

(**saw** needs no helping word)

William **had seen** a flamingo before.

(**had** helps the word **seen**)

We **have seen** flamingoes at the zoo.

(**have** helps the word **seen**)

The word **saw** needs no helping word.

The word **seen** always has a helping word:

has seen
have seen
is seen
are seen
was seen
were seen
had seen

A Use **saw** or **seen** to fill each space.

1 She ___   6 I have ___
2 They were ___   7 They ___
3 I ___   8 It is ___
4 She had ___   9 You ___
5 We ___   10 He was ___

B Which is right, **saw** or **seen**?

1 The wise men had ___ a bright star in the sky.

2 I ___ a merry-go-round at the fair.

3 Have you ___ the new car?

4 James ___ the football match from start to finish.

5 The policeman ___ a man breaking into a shop.

6 The robber was ___ by the policeman.

7 The robber did not know that he had been ___ .

8 I thought I ___ you at the party.

9 I knew I had ___ you before.

10 Fireflies are ___ at night.

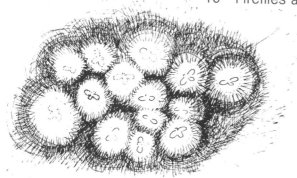

88